USE | YOUR
MIND
OR
YOU WILL
LOSE | YOUR
MIND!

USE | YOUR MIND
OR
YOU WILL
LOSE | YOUR
MIND!

Felicia Medlock

ARPress
ILLUMINATING IDEAS
EMPOWERING VOICES

ARPress
45 Dan Road Suite 5
Canton MA 02021
Hotline: 1(888) 821-0229
Fax: 1(508) 545-7580

Ordering Information:
Quantity sales. Special discounts are available on quantity purchases by corporations, associations, and others. For details, contact the publisher at the address above.

Printed in the United States of America.
ISBN-13:   Softcover   979-8-89330-528-9
              eBook   979-8-89330-530-2
              Hardback   979-8-89330-529-6

Library of Congress Control Number: 2024900546

DEDICATION

"GRAND KIDS"

JACOB AND PAIGE MY WONDERFUL GRANDCHILDREN. I HOPE A LESSON WILL BE LEARNED WHEN YOU BE A LEADER AND NOT A FOLLOWER ALWAYS LEAD THE WAY.

CONTENTS

This book is dedicated to the fifth generation of my family I want to shed light on our family's history and the real life issues you may or may not face in society today. This book contains advice from me to you. Think smart and become even smarter.

Jacob Anthony Joshua Feggins, Paige M. Bullock
Emerson, Noah, Ariana
Amiya, Elijah, Kaylee, Janiah
Adalynn Ava, Alayla , Ava, Serenity ,
Makayla, TaQuan Corinthian, De'Anthony Ziyon, Janiah, Elijah,
Chloe, Maddy, Jerimiah, Taylor, Victoria, Asha, and Asher

Grandson Jacob

My Family

oming from Mecklenburg County, a vast number of whites and blacks separated and could not be more devasted in the 1940's and 1950's. There were some still here to speak on the process of desegregation, how they made many sacrifices to see folks like you and me. We are still here to read and write about it. I was born in a city called Mecklenburg County South Hill Virginia. It was widely believed that African Americans were detached from whites in every shape form and fashion. For example blacks couldn't get the proper education as whites, Inez Boyd said, nor were they allowed to ride school buses. According to Lucille Hudson who witnessed schools where blacks sat in one room. Along with my mother and my Aunt Bessie explained to me the struggles they faced as children, so did others that are here to testify what they faced coming up.

South Hill Enterprise Love P. 2017,22-2. My Grand dad Andrews Feggins mail box and the well we drank from as kids, fresh water, not like the water we have today. In Mcklenburg.

Great grandma's grave, Bessie Feggins was born in 1885. My Mom and Aunts didn't get to meet her.

hrough it all Mrs. Lucille Hudson graduated from highschool in 1934, and after 43 years she was able to retire, but in the 1900 blacks situation was deplorable. This is a disgrace to the black race, Blacks were left with no vision of purpose. This book is to enlighten the new generation as to where they came from and the sacrifice our ancestors made to see a better way for us. Along with myself and the struggles I faced as a black woman not realizing the trials and tribulations I would endore as I grew into my adulthood. So, in your future be the best you can and don't let distractions or downfalls get you down. Can you imagine the separation? Blacks and whites even existed and still todays blacks are owed and fighting for equality. The pictures below shsow the people that held down the fort and made education possible. Proverbs 14:21 He who despiseth his neighbor sinneth; but he hath mercy on the poor, happy is he.

Beauty is Skin Deep

I was one of the ones born in Mecklenburg County Virginia along with my siblings and my mother and her siblings. This is my story, and this is my song, praising my savior all day long amen. In 1967, I was only one year old, As has been said, my mother wanted to keep me warm. So, she put a rocking chair by the stove and put me in it. Because the house was cold, and I was the baby of the family. For this reason, she asked my brother Harvey to watch me while she stepped away. In that time there weren't heaters, and the stove was not gas my parents had to throw wood in the fire to heat the stove, I was in a rocking chair, and I tragically rocked onto our iron stove.

My face was burned on the right side.

All in all, this wasn't just a burn this was a first-degree burn Coming up with the burn, on my face has been more than a challenge. In school, I was teased about my burn. I beat a girl up because she bothered me every day about it, and she pushed my buttons.

I felt shame about that incident. Although, I never thought I was pretty enough. There was a situation where a friend asked me to join her on a bus trip so I did, and I sat next to this guy, I was only about 15 and we talked, and he asked me, "what happened to your face? "I replied" I've had this on my face since I was one year old. To conclude, he said: any mark on a woman's face takes away the beauty in her, therefore, you will never be considered beautiful. Thus, he will never know how much that hurt my feelings, but I knew, God and I talked to him in the back of my mind I agreed with this guy but GOD, so I was like "yeah! you are right. I recently spoke to my brother about this after 54 years. He said he always blamed himself. I do believe your past plays apart in who you are and your attitude of how you treat others which is according to how you have been treated. My sister Trina was always the pretty one. If I did not meet the Lord and have a conversation with him, I don't know where I would be. In fact, I was blessed to be talented and smart. I have been blessed and able to do what most can't do! Therefore, if ever cannot answer your question correctly, I will get back to you with an answer. Undoubtedly, God has blessed me repeatedly and I was blessed with a voice. To summarize, I can and will continue to shout out to Him at any given time. Whenever things flow in my favor, I would say Thank you Lord amen.

1 Peter. 4:16 Yet if anyone suffers as a Christian, let him not be ashamed, but let him glorify God in that name.

The Life in my Hometown

First, I can only remember being about three years old and my mother brought us to Washington DC on a bus. She said she left because the house we stayed in in South Hill was so cold, and she had come to the city beforehand looking for jobs and my father stayed in South Hill Virginia. Later he came up and he was nearly frozen. The freeze bites were so bad, he had to get admitted to the DC General Hospital. Afterwards, the doctor had to amputate two of his toes. Meanwhile, in her suitcase, was all my mother owned.

My father Harvey Sr.

Gracious Grandma Martha Ann

Then, she hopped on a Greyhound Bus to Washington DC. Upon arriving, we went straight to the Adams Morgan area to a street called Ontario Road in Northwest. My Mother said it was a big welcome to see the bright lights of the big city. She had never seen so many lights before. My grandma's friend named Mr. Smith let my mother and her four children pile in His car from the bus station to Ontario Road, hence she said she would never forget him.

We stayed in a small apartment with my grandmother, My grandmother had some ways about herself! Oh, how my cousins Beaver, Monica and Lil John, Rocky, Linda, Kiki, Quincy, Marvin and Rachel.

We'd all laughed at her. Because when she said quotes like "Yall better stop wetting your hair going straight out in the cold you going to have arthritis! She was nosey too. Reminds me of myself because now I do the same thing! On corner of 18th street where she lived, every time we would walk pass her window, he would sit at the window watching everything in her view, telling us about it and we would say "Grandma somebody's going to shoot you one day because you always in that window (a Joke) Everyone knew and loved her and my aunt Vickie, They were such great women They passed away well over age 80, They lived great lives. My grandma's name was Martha Ann Feggins, She was well known, Everyone loved her.

Martha was my mom's name too, She was named after grandma

(mother) Martha Liz. First, Grandma married my grandfather Andrew Lee Feggins and they raised eight children. Their names were all Feggins, from the baby Naomi, Robert, Virgie, William, Richard, Eddie, Lee, Bessie and Mama Liz.

Momma Popcorn

However, they gave my mother a nickname, Popcorn. Moms said when she was eighteen,

she didn't have money for Christmas, The guys went into the woods and cut down a tree and she would string the popcorn on a string to make decorations for the Christmas tree. And everyone began calling her Popcorn.

Awesome Ancestors

Thus, my father was Harvey Gregory II and they called him Pop. I had two grandfathers Harvey Ruben Gregory The First and Roosevelt Feggins and two grandmothers Edith Alexander Gregory and Bessie Feggins and great Grand da and Grand ma Polly.

She was indentured over on a ship from Ireland, My aunt Inez said grand ma Edith was a sweetheart, Everyone loved her. She loved housework and cleaning, Reminds me of my sister Bee Bee. Also, at the time she spent working for the white folks, she also loved praising God. Reminds me of myself, from my father's side. My dad had two brother's named Ray Lee and James Eugene Gregory. We called him Uncle Purp. Both served in the United States Military (reminds me of my Brother Harvey Lynn Gregory III, who became Chief serving the Navy, also) After high school, my father's brothers Ray and James, along with their wives Inez Gregory and Betty Gregory, they migrated up North and resided in New York and New Jersey. Because down south had no transportation, and no jobs and nothing to do. However, Grandma

Edith's sisters my great Aunt's had relocated beforehand which gave them the ability to relocate, My Aunt Patsy in New Jersey, was a great woman who raised a lot of foster children, maybe ten or more. She also adopted a couple as well. She gave birth to my cousins Deborah, Delois and Jean Aunt Patsy and DeLois.

Picking Cotton and Tobacco

My mother and my Aunt Bessie explained to me the struggles they faced as little girls around the age of 13-15. They remembered having to pick tobacco and cotton on a field that the white man owned. My mother said by the time they finished their hands were black as tar. Also, sometimes they would put rocks at the bottom of the cotton to make it weigh more and they even urinated on the cotton to make it heavier to get more coins, while living in the county of Bracey Virginia. They had to skip school, not obtaining the proper education. They had to work to help survive living under a white man's roof and paying him rent.

Nevertheless, they would make around three dollars a day? a week? a month? or less which they were barely able to survive on back then living in poverty, and still not make enough money to eat. My Mother said she had to wash all the clothes and hang them on the line. When she seen the school bus, she would hide to avoid having her classmates see her missing school.

In conclusion, sometimes my mom said they would put rocks in the bottom of the cotton so that the bags weighed more. They even peed on the cotton.

Why Do I Have to call him Mister?

My grandfather was a carpenter, He helped build houses but that was only when work was needed. He had to fish to have food to eat. There were eight of my mom's siblings, so he would go hunting to kill rabbits and squirrels. They would must take turns to help skin and clean them. This was for them to have a meal. Clearly life was a struggle for our family's history. Adjacent to my grandmother how she would clean the white lady's house to make a little change.

Bessie said one day they had to run away and hide from the white man. The man that owned the store demanded they call him Mister. Aunt Bessie replied to granddad "Why do I have to call him 'mister' if he doesn't call me 'Miss Bessie" He doesn't call me Miss Bessie. Overall, she was to escape the small-town Bracey South Hill Virginia, while Grandma Martha still worked for the white lady?

My Grandmother rented a house there and she met a man by the name of Willie Simmons, he helped take care of the family and my Aunt Bessie had to help raise my other aunts and uncles. Nonetheless, she met a friend by the name of Tommy who lived in Washington DC, after finding Washington DC to be a better place with more opportunity for jobs and homes. Lastly came the relief from the slavery my grandmother followed Aunt Bessie and her siblings.

Grandma Martha and Granddad Andrew

Hebrews 13:5-6 Keep your life free from the love of money and be content with what you have for he has said "I will never leave; I never will forsake you" So when we can confidently say, "The Lord is my helper; I will not fear;" what can man do to me?

My Marvelous Mother a Spared

By the same token, my mother and father came together and found an apartment. Peripherally, I noticed my father worked every day to take care of his family. He was nice because he loved his family. I can remember he drank a lot; I remember my mother would run out the room. Only to say that my dad would yell at her, One day while arguing he critically he stabbed her in her side. There was so much blood! My mom was rushed to the hospital; we heard the ambulance. We were only children I believe I was about 6 years old. We were scared and bewildered. Overall, my father didn't remember. He felt sorry because his drinking habit was so intense, and he had no control of it clearly my dad didn't. My Aunt Inez said that her grandma told them, when he smacks you on one cheek turn your head and let him smack you on the other cheek and go somewhere and lock yourself in another room. As young black women this is the way they were geared to be. To stay in the situations as they arrive and act as if nothing happened.

Do not fear or be dismayed. Deuteronomy 33:27 My Mother knew that God would be her refuge and everlasting arms underneath.

8 is Enough!

When I was only three years old, we moved from the south to DC. My mother had five children Patricia, Anthony, Harvey, Trina and myself. My oldest sister Patricia stayed in Virginia with her dad's mother. After moving up to the city, a year later my mother had her sixth child, Bridgett who was born in DC at a hospital called DC General Hospital. My mother had Twins named Rochell and Shannel, which completed our family.,

Psalms 34:17 when the righteous cry for help the Lord hears and rescues them from all their troubles.

On the contrary, at the same time my dad's sister her name was Aunt Patsy, she lived in Patterson New Jersey, she showed concern, so she came to get my dad and he moved up north. After he left my mother according to my mother's best friend, Lilly Mae my father was my mother's first love and it was hard for her to get over him. Therefore, once my dad moved to New Jersey not long afterward, he found an apartment on 96th Street and Broadway in Manhattan, New York City. Spontaneously, we lived there a very short time. My mother started to realize the mental and physical abuse from my dad would never stop, neither would my dad stop drinking. As a result, she asked a friend to come help her, She wanted to relocate back to Washington DC. Mom called out for help, so she was rescued, and everyone knew she was abused before she left DC with her five children. The friend was Odell Battle who came to bring us back to DC and he never left my mother again. Tthey were married 46 years ago.

My stepdad Odell Battle on the left bottom.

1 Corinthians 13:4 Love is patient and kind love does not envy or boast; it is not arrogant or rude. It does not insist on its own way; it is not irritable or resentful; it does not rejoice at wrongful but rejoice with truth.

The truth is angels come is all shape form and fashion. My Mother never had to want for anything or live in fear again. Unfortunately, we received bad news that my father passed away of a heart attack, He was only 34 years old. Know that when you drink it has its effects on your body, so try not to abuse it. I was only seven years old I pray he did not suffer. Although, I took the passing of my dad hard because I didn't understand death and life. Despite of the passing of my dad, God knew he was destroying himself. Later Odell proposed to my mother, and they became united. He made a promise he would make her happy and safe from 1976 until today.

1 Peter 3;7 Likewise, husbands, live with your wives in an understanding way, showing honor to the woman as the weaker vessel, since they are heirs with you the grace of life, so that your prayers may not be hindered.

Sand Box

My mother and dad found an apartment in the Adams Morgan area on Kalorama Road northwest. The first people we met was Ester, Moe, Tanya and Ceclia the Middletons and the Louise The Turners and Tapers Sherry, Lulu, Smitty, Big and Tracey, Ms LuLu who live on Ontario Road in one of the biggest houses on the block, We went there to play. Their mother-Ms, Lu-had a large family like my mother. They were like our family. Those are our real sand box friends. In that manner we use to go on this hill on 17th street we called Snake Hill and play. This hill was all dirt, somewhere none of us were supposed to playing. We stayed in the building on Ontario Road with grandma Martha and My Aunt Bessie. Moreover, we were such little naïve children wanting to play together like children should at a young kinder garden age. I remember going to the day care called Morgan on Kalorama Road, We were only in pre-school.

Ephesians 5:28 In the same way husbands should love their wives as their own bodies, He who loves his wives loves himself.

The Rapport Ritz

Afterwards we lived in this medium size building called the Ritz, Everyone lived in this apartment building and we were like a big happy family. Everyone in the building became so close we called each other family. The first families we met when we came to the Ritz were the Barksdales, the Pryors, the Headspeths, the Masons, the Wise, and Caldwells. Although as a teenager with my big dreams and telling myself I wanted, To move to California when I turned 18, I always had a broad mindset. After moving to this building called Ritz, we heard of an organization called Jubilee.

We were around some pretty cool white people who came into the community and showed us much love by holding activities like cooking and sewing classes they also opened a recreational area where we could go after school. Moreover, we would also go on weekend camping trips to places like Moss Hollow located in Virginia.

Moss Hollow

This is where we could horseback ride and do all sorts of fun activities-some for girls and some for boys. Also, we went to day camp at a place called Camps Springs in Silver Spring, Maryland. What was interesting back then in the 70's we thought those areas were far away. We thought Maryland and Virginia was out of town, but the time of arrival was an hour or less. Also we went to a church on P Street Northwest with Jack. I remember so well by the grace of God.

I have loved church ever since; I knew that God was love and I kept that instilled in me. Overall, as time went on, life broadened with change. Consequently, I had big dreams for my life while watching my parents in the struggle. One wish was to have less children because I had so many siblings and I felt like I didn't want to have baby after baby. Living in the Ritz as child was a fun place to live until it turned into a small New Jack City like the. Movie that part is another story. Meanwhile, it seemed as if it was all a plan when the 80s hit and drugs were poured all over the city. They called DC Chocolate City and the

drug war was so bad we all moved to Rocky Mount North Carolina, We left the city because back then you could not trust nobody. The drug called crack cocaine came into cities all over the world. The plan was to destroy yourself. They were small capsules with red tops, and they were sold for 5 dollars and up. Washington DC had one of the best Mayors and the drug even took him down. The mayor has passed away but he was just another legend who the city will always honor.

Boss Lady got Baptized

Through it all, I found myself going to the church down the hill on Ontario Road (Adams Morgan) This was back in the days when life was easy being a kid. Along with a friend named Vernell I went to a church called King Emanuel Baptist Church and I was around 14 years old. We asked the Pastor by the name of Reverend Hunter to Baptize us, and he did.

King Emanuel Baptist Church

And then I was asked to go on a trip with a classmate. I was excited because the trip was to New York City. I was about fifteen years old. As we arrived, we were told we were sleeping in sleeping bags on the floor of the YMCA, I was shocked I said on the floor! I told her I didn't understand why they were calling us sheeps and lambs. To sum it up, it was a trip with her church, and it was a spiritual trip. I learned a lot about being a woman of God and I appreciated getting the opportunity to be a part of that trip. I realize that you are who you choose to surround yourself with, so stay prayed up and stay in good company of Christ- like folks, for this will be your way out and it will keep you.

Baptism the Christian spiritual rite of sprinkling water on to a person's forehead or of immersing them in water. This act symbolizes purification or renewal and admission into the Christian church. It's a symbol of commitment to God.

Let's Talk about Sex

We know the things that are right and wrong in life, but we choose a different path, As you grow with peer pressure of friends and the circle you choose to follow, (Don't be a follower be a leader) You are trying to fit in.

Friends I chose to be around were having sexual intercourse in junior high school and I was so scared to have a boyfriend, I thought about the physical education class in the eighth grade. The PE teachers taught us about two cells and an egg and a sperm that comes together during an intercourse makes a baby, It's funny because they don't teach that anymore. But it's also written in the bible: do not have sex before marriage. This is called fornicating when you have sex without a husband, so a lot of us coming up did not abide by God's word. Either we weren't taught, or we didn't listen.

1 Corinthians 7:1-2 It is good for a man not to have sexual relations with a woman. But since immortality is occurring each man should have sexual relations with his own wife, and each woman with her own husband.

Isaiah 26:3-4 Those of steadfast mind you keep in peace because they trust in you. Trust In the Lord forever for in the Lord God you have an everlasting rock.

However, it seems like back in the 50's and 60's that's what was expected from a woman, to have a lot of children and clean the house. Seems that's all women were supposed to do; sit at home with children and be a housewife. Hence, I'm smart in school on to the next level Its time for your junior high school prom with girlfriends. Currently every boy likes a girl or vice versa.

Therefore, for myself as an 8th eighth grader, I didn't want what to happen and was scared to indulge in sex. But one thing you will learn about real life is there are teenagers that do not follow the rules and you may be intimidated and want to have a boyfriend.

Otherwise, you are left out and feel alone, but never forget you have God to talk too in a time of need.

Mark 11:24 Therefore I tell you whatever you ask in prayer, believe that you received it, and it will be yours.

However, I had friends who started to indulge at a young age. Like my childhood friend Tracie had me under a lot of pressure peer pressure on. I kept in mine to myself. I'm going to make it out of high school, but I had friends and family members who quit school so never be intimidated and keep education first. They quit school, as early as junior high, Some are doing ok and some not so successful. I do know that you can be successful with a high school diploma. Tracie did well with her first son, She is a great mother now and she grew with her son as well and married happily ever after.

Remember some things in life I failed doing. My dreams, Was never

involved drug activities, so I still wonder how that became a part of my life. I have more time to think, and I look back at myself and I ask myself, What have I accomplished? For the most part, I didn't want to sit home old and grey. I wanted to gain the respect and leave a legacy for my children and grandchildren and their children.

1 Thessalonians 5;12-13 we ask you brothers to respect those who labor among you and over you in the Lord and admonish you, 13 and to esteem them very highly on love because of their work. Be at peace among yourself.

The Skate Life

Additionally, as children we had so much fun at different types of recreational activities in the city of DC, we grew up in the Adams Morgan area, back than we had the roller-skating rink my number one spot. Because we lived around the corner from Kalorama skating rink so and the little circle of friends as a result, we skated every day that we could. During the summer and every weekend in the same way. For the most part we called it day skating because at night the rink was for the older crowd. It was one of the best ways to exercise and get the cardio hence this was a healthy choice.

1 Timothy 4:8 For physical training is of some value, but Godliness has value for all things, holding promise for both the present life and the life to come.

Consequently, children would come to the Kalorama skating rink just to watch and hear good music, but for us we glide, Until this day most of us loved skating then, love skating now, We take pride in our ability to cruise around the rink, and we also took pride in our skating rink. Here are some great facts about this extracurricular activity. Our parents were able to give birthday parties on the weekend in the daytime for their children. Also, the adults host parties too. There was always something exciting going on at Kalorama skating rink. We loved skating couples listening to the slow jams, Triples consist of three people skating around the rink at a fast pace and women or men only, this is when you get to show your moves and groove at your own rhythm. In conclusion the skating rink became more of a hangout spot, meanwhile we found people coming to skate from Northeast, Southeast and Southwest. Maryland and Virginia started coming to the rink also. The older we got the skating rink became a target, There wasn't only skating, the organization started hosting shows and some bands performed.

Oh, I can't leave out the camera man! We could take a flick before the night was over. We even had late night skating. We loved skating so much we would skate all night long up until three in the morning. As children we weren't allowed to enter the building when they had adult activities. Some of the attractions and functions that the skating rink held drew attention from everywhere because it was such a great place to be. Simultaneously, the city thought that closing the doors of the rink would be a great choice for the residents who started to complain. Suddenly the skating rink closed. So, the city decided to turn the rink into a movie studio. Consequently, that didn't work out, so those doors were closed as well from what I see. Since then, the same skating rink building is now a Harris Teeter.

By the same token that was a big part of my life, and it saddens me that they closed the doors of the Kalorama skating rink . The skating rink once was recreation in Washington DC for children in the Adams Morgan area and it is gone forever. Hence there was violence and gun shots that over time started happening; that only meant there wasn't enough prioritized security. What was once called Chocolate City is now a minority. Now to skate children must go to Maryland.

Go-go Bands / Good Music

Overall, music is good for the soul, dancing or skating we had fun. In the 70's there was no such thing as a DJ. We had great Organ players and they played the organ so well, you would have thought you were listening to a record. Once again Black talented men who loved their instruments. Some of the guys that played the organ were even members of bands.

Speaking of bands, Washington DC was known for go-go bands. Now their bands originated out of Washington DC, but the bands are in all 50 states and known in different countries. For example Charles Louis Brown (Chuck Brown) was an American guitarist bandleader and singer. This was the first go-go band I ever seen. We called this legendary man the God father of Go-go. In the similar fashion, we called James Brown "the God father of soul." For those that don't know the meaning of go-go! Go-go is a subgenre of funk music developed around Washington DC Metropolitan area in the mid 1970's. Must go to Ben's Chili Bowl after the Go-go if they played in the Adams Morgan area. Now today Ben's Chili Bowl has expanded to more locations, although we lost the owner. Now today the wife has held the business down gracefully. We are honored to still have her.

Chuck Brown moved to DC from Gaston, North Carolina. When I tell you he took over DC with his band, if I can recall, he was in a jazz band first and he turned jazz into go-go. I'm not sure but if you hear his music, it's so mellow and smooth, you would have thought it's just another form of jazz in a go-go style. Coincidently, on the mic Chuck would tell you we came to have a good time, He did not like violence.

Chuck Brown, unfortunately, passed away on my mother's birthday May 16 at age 75. He will never be forgotten. In DC we have a Chuck Brown Park where they celebrate his birthday every year, and the city also honored him with a statue at Freedom Plaza the same as they did Dr. Martin Luther King. The moral of this story is his daughter KK Brown is still carrying on his legend with the Chuck Brown Band and here today, I would make it my business to see this great band because the band holds down the city. Also, Trouble Funk, Rare Essence, RE; Experience Unlimited E.U; Backyard Band, BYB, Vybe and Suttle Thoughts, to name a few. In my younger years, we enjoyed going to the go-go because this was the original lifestyle if you were from Washington DC.

I wasn't in that life, but if you didn't go to the go-go then you weren't a part of the circle. This circle could be a good circle or a bad circle for someone like me. I love to dance, I would dance anytime I heard music. This is another form of cardio that's good for the heart, When the go-go bands would host shows at decent places like this place called the Capital Center, you want to show up and show out. Because that was the good life with no violence, With high profile security you could enjoy yourself. Immediately after the go-go there was always a guy wanting to take you home or out for breakfast. There were certain groups or circles that would go to I-HOP for breakfast on a late night after the go-go.

The Masonic temple pic below was a spot-on U Street North West where Chuck Brown performed in Adams Morgan.

Masonic Temple was the spot for go-go bands like Chuck Brown.

Almost Raped

Unfortunately, I was almost raped before leaving a go-go. No means No. Men don't seem to understand that. Granted, he offered me a ride home and thought, because he was in a nice car and he was giving me a ride that he could ride me, I offered him gas, but he didn't want gas he wanted ass. I want to give his name, but I would not want to be sued. This is to say; be careful who you hang out with and beware of your surroundings. On the contrary, I was a young adult, never was I scared because I only feared God. When I thought I was grown and I was young minded, and I wanted the grown mentality. Despite the lifestyle I chose coming up as a young adult, I prayed to God every step of my way. For this reason, never give up on God. Because God will never give up on you. And yet I have walked the streets all times of the night alone and made it home safely. Because I walked with prayer no matter where I went or what I was doing, I prayed to God to have a better life. This is something very important to teach yourself and your children because without God you have nothing.

Romans 8:18 The pain that you've been feeling, can't compare to the joy that's coming.

Recreation for Children in Adams Morgan

nother great activity we enjoyed was the Happy Hollow children's swimming pool on Champlain St northwest. However, Happy Hollow swimming pool was one of the first pools around for us as little children to swim in in the Adams Morgan community.

In the 70's we had lots of recreation for children in the community we grew up in. When 18th Street and Florida avenue started becoming like New York strip I said to myself this area is not a good area to raise children because there are too many adult activities here that will allow children to start drinking alcohol. Seems like now, the area has bar and grills on every corner.

For the most part we had the Ontario movie theater located at the corner of 17th and Columbia Road. We had a local place to see movies that now a condominium building with balconies. Another movie theater was the Embassy movie theater on Florida Avenue.

Also, there was a corner store called Tic Toc located on 18th St and Kalorama Road where we could buy candy after school the owner named Mr. Pile was the nicest man you could ever meet. He let us get what we needed, and we could pay later. He passed away, He was such an awesome guy May he rest in peace.

In addition on Columbia Road we had two arcade rooms. One was next to the long term McDonald's that's been there longer then I can remember. My sister Trina, Nay Nay, my brother Harvey, Anthony and myself along with others we would head there to play arcade games and see who was the best. Once again that spot is now a restaurant or club. We had another Arcade spot on Ontario Rd. and Columbia Rd across from the Metro liquor store. My brother Anthony, we call him Bro, oversaw this game room, It was a blessing to have a brother in charge because he would let us get free games sometimes when we were low in quarters. The Adams Morgan area has changed so much However.

Still enjoying the life of Washington DC partying and having fun enjoying everything that comes by rather it's a Live Go go band or a celebrity so one day we were on 18 and Colorado Road standing at the corner of my grandmothers house and here comes a limousine up the street and the guys were hauling out of the sunroof screaming fuck the police and we were like who in the world would be so rude to The city saying words like that with no remorse and one of my friends yell out the window and said that's 2Pac that is the guy that sang Brenda's got a baby and he was a celebrity and they told us to come to the club called the Kilimanjaro which was on California Street right from my grandmothers house so we went to the Kilimanjaro. Overall they talk to us they liked us we like them and they told us they were going to be staying at a hotel on G St. downtown DC by the convention center and they asked us to come to the hotel , so after the show at the Kilimanjaro we're headed down to the hotel the reason we went to the hotel because they told us if we can dance we can be a part of their next video and for someone like me who always wanted to be in the spotlight I was like sure I can dance and I would like to be in the video video so we had it down to the hotel and we got into the room and they told me to show them what I can do so I jumped up on the dresser and kicked off my shoes and I had on some stockings and leggings and I started to do some Michael Jackson moves on top of the dresser as I proceeded to do my little dancing throwing them that I can dance I dived off the big dresser and did a forward Ro went to the bed and I checked his manager and the four head really hard and they all stopped and everybody Paul and they all looked at me and was like 0h shit.....l and they grab the pillows off of the bed and they started pillow fighting me hitting me in my head with the pillow so hard I was like I'm out of here and grab my things and I wanted to go and I told my friends this girl and they did not want to go and they were very upset With me because they wanted to stay. The moral of the story is it doesn't matter who you meet and how great they are always know that if you feel certain senses within your own soul that you know is not right follow your senses they.

Braiding Hair

I had another legend in my life. My Godmother. Her name was Ms. Mattie She owned the convenience store in the best the location. Was on 17th and Columbia Rd. northwest, This store was like the first stop after school. I was a young entrepreneur so long ago as a child and didn't know it. I used to help her as a cashier a childhood friend and myself. Ms. Mattie taught us much about how to franchise a business. If we had listened more and followed her footsteps and said NO to drugs, our path in life would have been successful early on.

As a child I would be her assistant and, on top of learning about inventory in the store. I would stand behind her and braid her hair in a fan? same style every time because, Ms. Mattie got so many compliments on her hair every time. Out of all the years I did her hair she never wanted a different style while she was on the register for years. She would pay me to braid her hair and help close her store at night. Sometimes I would go with her to wholesale stores to get the inventory. I must say I have that same entrepreneur mind I had as a kid. I learned from her. She was my Godmother. Ms. Mattie moved to Washington DC from Savannah, Georgia, and opened at least seven stores. She was a very smart and intelligent black female who passed away as a legend. She did well in her life and her success from all her stores was hard work and dedication. So, when you surround yourself with positive energy you are liable to have a positive outcome in your life.

Romans 8:31 What, then shall we say in response to these things? If God is for us, who can be against us?

2 Peter 3:9 The Lord is not slow in keeping his promise as some understand slowness. Instead, he is patient with you not wanting anyone to perish, but everyone to come to repentance.

Friends

After school myself and a childhood friend Maria, we'd play outside doing flips, cartwheels and walkovers. The older men would challenge, asking us to do flips from the corner of Euclid Street to the corner of Fuller Street, and they would pay us money. Those were fun times in life, when you think about it, we learned to make money at a very young age, and we made it honestly with our talent. My friends also happened to be my children's God mothers.

Deborah and Stephanie, they helped when I wanted a break as their father should have. My friend Stephanie, she is smart, I like the way she would in life. She said NO to drugs. She was one who bought her first car at a young age, and she didn't want to get pregnant.

Glamour Girls

Between her and I we would cut our own hair and get compliments almost every day. Stephanie was the glamur queen she liked make up more than I back in the day. She learned how to put-on makeup very early, as if she was a makeup artist. We were close friends since we were seven years old and that's been more than forty years ago, Naturally, we still hold that bond until this day. We thought we were like salt and pepper because she was light, and I was dark. Having someone to talk to, I could always count on her. Overall, you couldn't tell us nothing thought we were the glamur girl's. Life looks better when you step out the door looking like a star, so we would do our best.

Proverbs 18:24 some friends play at friendship but a true friend sticks closer than one's nearest kin." Know who your friends are.

As you get older, you want to have as many friends as a child. You think you have so many friends, but you can only trust a few.

Proverbs 27:5-6 Better is open rebuke than hidden love. Wounds from a friend can be trusted, but an enemy multiplies kisses.

Make sure you know the meaning of friends because friends have bonds and some sort of affection mutually. Friends show support of one another inspire them and speak highly of them so watch your friends. They are not to speak down on you even when you're down, Their job is to lift your spirits and make you feel better inside and out. Sort of like the song says ("Friends how many of us have them?")

Friends are trustworthy, empathetic, selfless and team players.

There was never a time I would call her I and tell my visions. She would inspire me, She never once thought I couldn't do whatever I visualized. She would say. "Pat, you can do it." The same way I would tell her that she can do better in life for whatever she was thinking.

Stephanie has earned her Doctorate in Theology. She has mastered in the word of the Lord; I love her for that.

I must admit Stephanie's mother, Mrs. Stella preached to me so many times about drugs and what God didn't like about harming yourself. I can remember I told her I wanted to kill myself. I had smoked some marijuana that was mixed with PCP I said Ms. Stella, I don't want to live anymore, She took me in the living room and sat me down and told Stephanie to get that holy water out of her room she prayed over me and said in the name of the Father Son and the Holy Spirit I rebuke the devil from your soul . I believe the holy water worked and her prayer. Likewise, I have another close friend name Redina we graduated from Woodrow Wilson high School Together. Redina studied Theology and so did her sisters.

Angelica, Redina and myself

Ms. Francis Seaborne raised some awesome women because studying the word of the Lord puts you with a clear mindset, We should all know as much as we can about Christ. I do believe Joseph Canty my girlfriend Redina's husband led them to follow Him. Consequently, Joe became a Leader easily thirsty for the Lord. He is an inspiring man with a humble soul. In fact, my husband says he sounds just like Dr. Martin Luther King when he speaks the word on Sundays, Besides her family, along with her two girls Joel and Joy, have been fortunate to feed the homeless and they did great things for the community before they relocated. Like I said before surround yourself with positive energy and make sure you're not dealing with the devil because the devil comes in many shapes forms and fashion.

Scared to have Sex

When I was 16, I really thought to feel I was grown as the average girl should, but I still wasn't able to take care of myself. In that manner my friends thought they were young adults. As well they had boyfriends and they were having sexual intercourse I knew the right thing to do was wait. To rephrase, we were doing our best to succeed and not slip and fall in the trap of the welfare system. Whereas most young girls have a baby before they are 15, by doing so as young mothers they continue to deal with boys who are immature and don't know their way in life and to butter it up, disclaim their child, and don't help with the child. In conclusion this led to a much further issues because psychologically with a mind that is not fully mature then you start making poor discissions. At that time the mindset changes and you have the baby without all your education and barely making great things happen for yourself, Not only does the baby daddy want to come around and try to help you with the child, but he wants a blood test to prove the child is his. Going forth the baby is growing and so are the teenagers, and some didn't finish their education and start smoking marijuana not knowing one drug leads to another.

So now at that time: You look around the city with a lot of young girls pushing strollers and your dreams have crashed and you need so much more help. You haven't finished school and now you must find childcare, and you have parents that try to help as much as they can by babysitting, and you must join the welfare line and the WIC program for the baby's formula and food stamps. So you ask yourself when will you catch a break? To sum it up, the government allows small programs with computer trainings that are free and you find yourself taking trainings and still can't get a job over the pay of entry level employment, but what I've learned through it all to stay prayed up and one day things will get better providing you continue to take care of your child and provide the best care for them to your knowledge and one day the Lord will bless you with a better life.

Romans 3 it states stay thirsty for the Lord and you will be blessed abundantly.

1 Corinthians 1:2 NLT

I am writing to God's church in Corinth, to you who have been called by God to be his own holy people. He made you holy by means of Christ Jesus, just as he did for all people everywhere who call on the name of our Lord Jesus Christ, their Lord and ours

Having Sex Outside of Marriage

Though it all in so although you are allowing the love of a man outside of marriage and you give them your temple and you know it's not right, you do it anyway. As a result you want a man that loves you for you. He tells you he wants to marry you, Believe him You will do anything to keep him your baby daddy is no longer in the picture and this is your second boyfriend. You thought was a good idea to have sex and boom you get pregnant again. Not only can you not take care of the first child, but now the second child is here and the second baby father does the same thing. While living in the city some guys didn't learn the proper morals of life, so the lack of fatherhood is natural for them.

Corinthians 1:2 provides you with the knowledge to love one another and love is joy. Philippians 4;6 Do not be anxious for nothing, bur in every situation and God will provide.

One thing I had to learn is that though you have hard times, when you think you can't make it, there is a God and I learn to have faith that God will see you through. In the long run, I was able to raise my beautiful children Gary and Porsche and teach them. However, rather they follow or not, I did my job as a mother and I'm proud of myself.

For the love of Gymnastics Of course I'm in the middle

Girls Gymnastics

(Left to Right) Rena Colman, Lisa Robinson, Tersa Bennett, Shane Ivy, Ikereuwem Inyang, Marilyn Credle, Adowa ... Myra Credle, Martha Affora, Pearl LeGrand, Angela Artis, Karessa Buchanna, Teresa Bennett, Valora Sh...

Some made it and some didn't make it to high school, I was one of the fortunate ones to make it to high school I was very athletic and very talented a jack of all trades. However, I loved gymnastics the most! I couldn't wait until the Olympics came on and I would say to myself, I'm going to be just like Nadia Comaneci! She was a five-time Olympic gold medalist, and she was the first the score a perfect 10 at the age of ten in 1976. Subsequently, I went to Dunbar, which was a school out of the zone where I lived, but my goal was to join the best gymnastics team in the high schools, Once I attended Dunbar in my tenth-grade year, Because I was one of the best gymnasts in junior high school, I received several trophies for gymnastic competitions, One of my dreams was to be a gymnast and go to the Olympics I am here to tell you: follow your dreams, no matter how hard it seems. Until this day I still do gymnastic move because I believe that dream wasn't for fulfilled. Between me, my brother Bro and Darnell thought we could out flip one another. I found Dunbar had the best equipment but no team. There wasn't much I couldn't do I loved helping others and doing all kind's of things in school I was most popular. I was on the cheerleading team temporarily at Dunbar senior high and on the gymnastics team; also in ROTC.

My brother Bro and Darnell
(The Gymnast)

I love to Sew

After transferring to Woodrow Wilson senior high, throughout high school I became a good seamstress. I started sewing at Dunbar and Lincoln Junior high school. I loved to sew like my mom, I made my own prom gown. We were told that if we wanted a gown for the prom our home economics Teacher would charge us three hundred dollars and she would make it for us. Of course, my motto is "Why pay for something when you can do it yourself?" So, I decided to go to the fabric store and buy the material by the yard and get a Vogue pattern and make my own gown. Through it all, I was an A student in sewing but because I chose to make my own gown Mrs. Hunter the sewing teacher gave me a final grade a D.

Being a Fashionista

I was proud of my gown, and it turned out to be a red with white bows from the waist straight to the heel of my feet and the bows were very large and as they went to the floor, they got smaller and smaller, hence, to let you know.

Philippians 4:13. I can do all things through God Christ that strengthens me.

In high school I loved to dress like a punk rocker, and I was into the latest fab. Sometimes, I would stand in stores grabbing Vogue magazine looking at fashion, in Paris, Italy and so on. I am told I'm my mother's child.

My mother always looked good and matched with accessories with whatever she wore. But one thing I can say about my mom is she gave way lots of clothes and she would feed you when you were hungry. And I would do the same.

1 Samuel 16;7 But the Lord said unto Samuel, do not look on its appearance or the height of his stature, because I have rejected him. For the Lord sees not as man sees man, look on the outward appearance, but the Lord looks on the heart.

I love to go to Georgetown and shop. Most of us who went to Jackson Reed High School which was previously called Woodrow Wilson President high school, loved to shop.

A former President this school was in the higher-class area and there is here I met multicultural students for example Chinese, black, white, Ethiopians and so on. My first school of choice was Dunbar majority blacks where I barely sew any white students. In addition, I was catching three buses to school every day and he S2 to 16th and P Street NW and transfer to the P Street bus to New Jersey Avenue and P Street to Dunbar. At that time Dunbar was a newly built school in 1981. At the present time the school has been remodeled again. The front is now the back, and the back is the front.

However, my sister-in-law Sandy said that when she attended Dunbar, she only could wear skirts and the only time you could have worn pants was at gym. The school was located where MM Washington is on P st, also the street cars was only ten cents to ride. Washington DC have street cars again now 2022 and its free the streetcar only runs from Union Station to 24th and Benning Road.

The life in the Streets of D.C.

The above picture is what 14th Street Northwest looked like and the store called Woolworth is where my friend's mom worked most of her life in her younger days a shot out to Mrs. Katherine Washington. Most that have been gone from the area of Adams Morgan know that you can find Ms. Katherine because she is still there. My friend Tracie and I would always say our Mothers were born the same year and they both had 8 of us. However, it bothers me how the seniors have made their way to survive, but the benefits to help seniors are unacceptable. The District should be able to grandfather the elderly in with the cost of the economy in the city, The rent is sky high. My major was Gerontology. I feel when you are too old to speak up for yourself there should be someone with a louder voice to speak for you. Once you're 80 and 90 years old, if you're like my mother, she just wants peace. If I would have studied more, I would have kept Gerontology as my major. I went to a very strategic school called Maryland University and the classes were a lot of strain on me once again I stopped going. Just to say keep going, Don't give up on your dreams.

John 5:4 for whatever is born of God overcome the world - our faith.

While out and about with not only one child, but now you have two, the life of Dc streets only got tough. Since I was still at home with my parents, I was trying my best but it all crashes. At the point of making entry level money and if you put your child in day care you will have to pay the daycare, with the little change I made. However, the system is designed to help you which is the welfare system. It could be at your advantage or disadvantage only because at this point I looked at the picture different. I'm not saying I had an advantage for a lower income apartment, because that wasn't the case. I never lived in a Section 8 apartment, Most cities were are so behind back then and they still are for those type of apartments. More so, I had friends that was called to receive a lower income apartment. Not only did they have a section A apartment. Again, young women with great potential to have a set back their future only because they decided not to get out of the system that is designed to help you or fail. Equally important our young men suffer also with the drugs poured into the District and they aren't fortunate to get stability.

Thus, they began to go to war against one another. Even when they aren't involved in drugs, my family suffered a loss of my nephews, Anthony and Joshua, who were gunned down on the streets of the District. By a menace to society who should have never been released for five murders prior.

Psalms 73:28

But is it good for me to draw near to God: I have put my trust in the Lord God that I may declare all thy works.

At this point in my life after high school I had a great in-school program job with GSA (General Service an Administration) working as n administration assistant, however I failed in this position because I was fresh out of high school. I thought I was smart enough to not start college and attend a trade school, the National Institute of Cosmetology, to become a professional Hairstylist.

However, I was stuck on stupid after thinking a boy loved me and we could live happily ever after. Life turned because I thought I loved him. Unfortunately, this one introduced me to drugs which is marijuana and enbalming fluid.

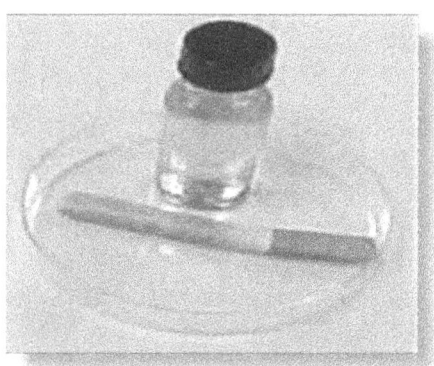

Therefore, I advise all younger generations to stay away from all drugs because it leads to poor decisions. I started arriving to work late. This was a government position. I didn't know the meaning of being on time when I desired to do wrong. I wasn't in the right state of mind. I never did such thing at work, but when you indulge after work you have consequences. As a result, I did not have a job anymore. Fortunately, most of the neighborhood can say I was doing their hair. My blessed hands have touched a lot of heads I must say. (smile) I would sit at home making over five hundred dollars a week braiding, perming, and cutting hair. Once again, a successful young black female with great potential for herself and having a lot of wasted time doing ridiculous things to ruin her life.

This is crack cocaine that hit the streets of Washington DC heavy in the 80's. Question is, how did these drugs get in the hands of the young people.

Nehemiah 8:10

Do not grieve, for the joy of the Lord is your strength.

Exodus 15:2

The Lord is my strength and my song he has given me victory.

Thus, all that time could have been spent on getting the knowledge to be great. So again, try to find love when you're old enough and watch out who you choose to engage in sex with, because you want someone who is going to marry you and be by your child's side, and you want them to also love them unconditionally. Learn their morals and values and make sure they love their parent. I mean love as in take care of their mother because if they take care of her, they will more than likely take care of you. The devil works in many ways. This is how the world works, When you are lifted, God is there to hold your hand. Don't stray away.

1 Peter 2:17

Honor all men. Love the brotherhood. Fear God Honor the king.

I do know I have feared God all my life and not feared man with the faith that's was instilled in me. I know he has shown me the way the truth and the light. I know in my hardship times; I was blessed to have beautiful children. With my son and daughter, Gary and Porsche, the agony was real. I taught them as much knowledge as I have learned in my lifetime. I was growing with them so I knew that they would have the proper education they needed, and so should you. Having education will help you in every angle of your life, Instead of following the crowd you should lead the crowd. Education is the key - this doesn't mean you know everything, that glory goes to God.

Matthew 5:16

Jesus said let your light shine before others, so that they may see your good works and give glory to your father in heaven.

Having proper education will mean the world to you and your parents. (I don't know) Father I pray that each person reading this book is learning something, or it helps to build their confidence as a person because if they took the time to read, then I know they have the power to succeed.

Proverbs 14:34

Righteousness exalts a nation but sin is a reproach to any people.

If anyone had the right to look down on others it was Jesus, but he didn't. With that being said, I was bitter with my children's fathers, but I still had to respect them for helping me produce the beautiful children I gave birth to. The same as all we must show respect for one another. I realized that the only thing in life is to make yourself happy first, and then you can tolerate others, but when you are bitter inside you show anger, You will take it out on others. Therefore, you will have to be treated for anger management.

In Antioch, Peter was looking down on gGentiles because someone said they weren't as good as him. Paul put a stop to it. Jesus ate with sinners and didn't look down on anyone.

Growing up with my children

As you grow in adulthood you will realize that every man is out for themselves, but this is not what Jesus wanted he wants us to show love for one another.

Granted, raising two children who are now awesome with more than one degree, highly educated I must say I am the proudest of them all. I even successfully accomplished my degree and had the pleasure to graduate with my son, Only God.

My son Gary was the man of my house in their early childhood age. I had him lifting heavy items at an early age when we were relocating as if he was a man already; he was only about 12. But he was a strong boy, along with his sister by his side. My daughter would watch me clean up and she had a child size broom, and she would do the same and start cleaning too and try to cook. Overall, she would sit right beside me when I had to do hair outside the home. At the present time she has followed my footsteps. She's doing hair which was a natural profession for the both of us.

There were days I caught the bus with my children. I recall taking them with me to apply for jobs. I told them one day at the mall to do what I do. While filling in the blank application. I would give them an application, too. They were way too young to get a job, but I taught them early. So regardless of what happens to me, they would know how to prepare themselves for the world. At that time, they were like 8 to 10 years old.

Sometimes the cycle can go on and on. For instance, some aren't taught to be a parent, yet I decided to have a child. I only can teach a child what I know. Centrally, if I had taken the time to learn how to be a parent first, there is ample enough room to teach my child what I've learned.

Proverbs 22:6 Train up a child in the way they should go and when they grow old, they will not depart from it.

Remember, you may consider having a child but learn and be financially stable. This message is to the young males and females. Make sure you know your mate, be concerned who you choose to share your temple with because it can be ruined. Most guys don't know how to raise a child and neither did I. Hence your child will grow in their feelings, without the presence of their father.

Ephesians 6:4 Fathers, do not provoke your children to anger, but bring them up in the discipline and instruction of the Lord.

I had a friend. He introduced my children to his mom. She was a great belssing. When you trust in the Lord with all your heart and lean not to your own understanding.

Proverbs 3:5-6 Trust in the Lord with all thine heart; and lean not unto your own understanding. In all thy ways acknowledge him, and he shall direct your path.

As a result, all I wanted was to live and see my children accomplish greatness in their lives. That's all any mother wants for her children because, success is the key. Her name was Alma and she was an angel in disguise which means it was the most difficult time in my life, it was obvious. She was an angel sent from God with a heart of gold. Alma passed away at 75. We will always love and miss her. While you are reading this, remember God is watching over you, keep the faith deep in your soul. Faith means having a firm conviction in something or someone. All you need is faith the size of a mustard seed and God will take care of you, amen.

My Siblings

verall, we are survivors, from my oldest sister Patricia Ann 62 years young. She was raised with her nana in her younger days spending a lot of time in church. She taught me the Lord's Prayer when I was 10 years old, and I wrote it repeatedly until I got it. She went to college in Raleigh, North Carolina and began her career and married my brother-in-law, Wilbert. And living happily ever after with two children and a grandson.

Then my oldest brother Anthony, 61. He had two children and never married. He loves to do what he wants to do.

My brother Harvey, 59 retired Chief in the Navy. He is the Monarch of the family. He married Carol with two children and 5 grands. Trina, 57, she had four boys and three grands, She is still finding her way and I believe God is keeping her until she can put her faith in Him.

Bridgett, 51 she got married to Troy and has three children pursuing her career in Norfolk, Va.

Twins, Rochell, 46 she retired from the Navy. She had a successful career. She married Ron with two kids.

Shannel 46, married to Chuck with two kids, and she is retired. The throne my brother acquired he passed down to her. She was a Chief in the Navy as well, with a successful career.

And a Godbrother Louis and sister Sheila. God, nothing can take us down. I am thankful to have 7 siblings and two that spares my mother took in as her own. We have survived the battle, but the battle is not yours, it's the Lords. Prayer is everything. Nevertheless, we are still in a battle, America has been hit by a many viruses.

Romans 8:31 If God be for me, who can be against me?

Family is like branches on a tree, we all grow in different directions, but the root remains the same.

Double - Dutch Twins

The Twins, Some know them as the twins, They jumped Double Dutch with Ms. Thornton from our elementary school HD Cooke

and had the pleasure to travel to Russia and make the front page of the Washington Post, while they were only in sixth grade. Oh of course they got that part from me. I jumped double - Dutch in elementary too, along with my partner Maria Pryor. We received several trophies also.

My In-laws

I have 8 additional siblings in my family, which is Curtis 82, Derek, 67, Arron, 65, Karen 70, Darlene 63, married Mike, Charlene Darryl 63 (Twins) and Johnnie May. Overall, I can't say one bad thing about my in-laws, because they loved me as if I were born into the family. One good thing I can say about the Medlocks is they love to work.

Ordinarily, my sister-in-law Charlene has made me feel extra special from A-1 day, because every year on my birthday she gives me a gift nicely wrapped in purple paper (she knows I love purple) also with a cake, card and balloons. In other words, she has been doing this routinely for me before she even knew me well, over 22 years ago and never missed a year.

Know that God is love and know your worth so you can be loved the same way(amen). Inspite of the ups and downs, life may take you through but with faith in God and a prayer you'll never know the angel could be walking right by your side throughout your journey in life.

Genesis 2:20 -25 The family is the foundation institution of society

ordained by God. It is constituted by marriage and is composed of persons related to one another by marriage, blood, or adoption. The family is a fundamental institution of human society.

Meeting My Soul Mate

In 1998, I worked for District of Columbia Public Schools Transportation, which is where I presently work, and I met a guy by the name of Lockup. I asked him two questions. What is your real name? and why they call you Lockup? Hence, he replied because. I was a good basketball player in the Army and when I had to shoot the ball, I locked the ball in, so the team gave me the name Lockup.

So, he said my name is Darin Medlock, I said wow I've never met a guy named Darin before. After meeting him my daughter was only ten and my son was twelve he became by boyfriend. He was still in the Army. I knew he was the guy for me because he spoke highly of his mother Dorothy Graves Medlock may she rest in peace. She passed in 1996 before I could have met her the only Mother-in-law I will ever have in this lifetime. Also, he spoke highly of his father Tiny Medlock at the time his father was living. He acted just like his dad, who of course spoke on his wife as well.

When my father-in-law met me and he learned my ways he told me, I was a humdinger. I laughed sigh? I didn't know what that meant!

He said I was just like his daughter Charlene who is now my sister-in-law. Hence, he called her a humdinger too. Oh my God!

To sum it up, Darin and I became great friends. Equally important, on my birthday November 13, 2001, standing in the presence of his dad in the living room, he said "Will you marry me?" I was shocked! I said "if you get on your knee likewise," we laughed, he kneeled and proposed to me.

I was so excited, all I could do was look up and say, "Thank you, Lord." He completed our family on March 9, 2002, on his birthday. We are still united. Twenty-two years later until this day he has made me as happy as he could. He is my soul mate, he said "happy wife happy life."

I could not ask the Lord for a better man. Oh, just to say, I would not marry him until he got saved. So we went to church, and he gave his life to Christ.

Spontaneously, on his birthday, March 9, 2002, we were married at National Wesleyan Church. We had a nice simple wedding and no reception. We only donated to Pastor Ira Taylor and the singer; in fact, we bought flowers from a friend Angelica she owned a flower shop in Brentwood, Md. My hubby Darin is now retired Army and retired Post Office. He has set a great example overall and has been a great Father to our children. Believe that God will lead you. Thus, you don't have to understand why the things that happens to you but please believe that God has something in stored for you. You gotta believe!

I took a trip to visit my brother-in-law, Arron Medlock. He was blessed to buy property in the south about 20 miles or less from Mecklenburg County, where I was born. Let me end this story in a great way. I woke up Sunday morning and said I'm going to find me a church down here to attend so, I went to Lawrenceville Baptist Church. I walked into the church. The love was real, Some looked and some stirred, but I was comfortable in the house of the Lord just to look around and I was the only black person in the whole church. I felt like a star because afterward these awesome folks wanted to know my name and where I was from. Coincidently, they knew my maiden last and one of their names was the same as mine. Her name was Patsy. (sigh)

Thankful For Our Mother

I want to give a special shout out to My one and only mother. She was born in 1943 in Mecklenburg County. She was spared with 8 of us. We will never know the thoughts that have crossed her mind although she will be 80 years young next year and I ask lots of questions. While raising all of us her grapples couldn't have been any harder with the Lord on her side. I must say to you listen and learn from the wise overall, they do have all the answers.

Felicia E. Medlock

I love you

God is love

"Be great"

Words are image containers you can get a picture from someone's words. Soar my Scholars Soar...